ILLUSTRATIONS BY: SAMANTHA TRECO
@SAMANTHATRECO
SVKTRECO@GMAIL.COM

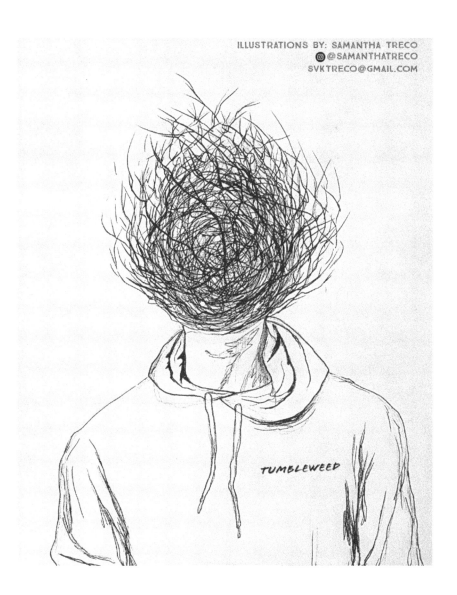

Bad Poetry

Vol. 1
Tumbleweed

Alejo A Rodriguez

PAGE PUBLISHING, INC.
Conneaut Lake, PA

First originally published by Page Publishing 2021

ISBN 978-1-64701-975-4 (pbk)
ISBN 978-1-64701-976-1 (digital)

Printed in the United States of America

Dedicated to
God
My Family
My Mother
My Circle
Role Models
Page Publishing

Rest in Paradise
Tia Morena
Tia Martha
Tio Mario
Carmen
Abuelo
Junior
Alejo
Yael
and
my dog, Bruce

CONTENTS

First Poem 11

Preface...13

I Write Because 15

Tumbleweed...16

Fork in the Road 17

Commitment 18

Date...20

Weather..21

Just Know 22

Sleepless Nights..23

A Letter to My Father (Part 1)...................................24

LOVE 27

Fisherman 28

Love?..29

Decisions..30

Loss for Words 31

Knock, Knock...32

Supposed To 33

Feelings 34

Me 35

Losing Battle 39

Fight 40

Suicidal Thoughts 41

Pain..42

In Love..43

Butterflies...44

Mind My Business 45

Pulled Over 46

Stuck..47

IDK 48

Scared 49

Perseverance 50

Her 52

Fatherless..54

Cheating 55

True Colors 56

Addiction 57

Saying Goodbye 59

Why..60

Still Remember..61

Who? 63

My Father's Child..64

Man's Best friend 65

Can't Be 66

30..68

Mommy...69

The Game 70

Behind Closed Doors 72

Text...74

Thank God for ~~Tragedy~~ 77

God, I Got Some Questions 79

Family Feuds 80

Mine 82

Thoughts of the Dead 83

BRUCEEEE..84

Engagement 86

Don't Trust You 87

Death...88

That Girl..89

Countless 90

Love Yourself...91

Ocean Floor 92

God...93

Suicide 94

The Call...95

My Mother..97

Fatherhood 98
Unlock 99
Strings 100
You Hate Me 101
Your Worth 103
I Can't Be 104
Thank You 105
Don't Forget 106
What If 107
Connected..108
Not My Fault 109
Love Me 111
Karma 112
The Bill...113
Some 114
Wanted 115
New York, New York 116
Who's Really American...117
Burning Bridges 118
The Irony...119
Caged Open 120
Living Dead 121
Money...123
If You Knew… 124
Fighting...126
Don't Love Me Like That 128
I Met a Man..129
Rough Times 130
The End 131

FiRST POEM
1/27/95

the dog ~~ran~~ aFter the Cat

the dog did not like the
Cat but the Cat did like
the mouse. ~~but~~ The dog did
not bother He

Preface

This Book

This book gives you a look into my feelings
Feelings I rarely show
People tell me I should express myself more
and I do on paper with words, not vocally
So here it is
a book on things
that have happened to me
someone I know
or something I saw
that bothered me to the core
Furthermore, this book is me
being as vulnerable as I can possibly be
whether I sell a copy or not
It's not about that
I really don't care
I don't consider myself a poet
Why? Because I honestly
don't think I'm as talented as I should be to call myself one
But regardless I'm going to publish a collection of words
that allowed me to sleep when I couldn't
A collection of words
that allowed me to express myself
when I couldn't express
my thoughts and feelings
to anyone in particular
This collection of words
turned into a book

showing you my growth
my dreams
my fears
and my flaws
It shows the side of me
unrecognizable to most
Enjoy the ride
It's a roller coaster
There's no order
no plan
no expectations
Just Polaroids
of life experiences
through my eyes

I Write Because

I write poetry
to release the buildup of emotions
I develop internally
Without this release you can guarantee
the increase of less sleep
Which would ultimately
just give me added stress and grief
So a brief dive
into the deep array of thoughts
gives my heart and mind
the ability to stay at bay
Allowing me
to keep the *in* away
from my *sanity*

Tumbleweed

How I roam down
these lonely dirt roads, deserts, and streets
Unaccompanied
Humbled
At once having it all
So young, so naive
Now I am rolling around aimlessly
But I've been taught that life
is a marathon, not a sprint
I've learned that there are good times and bad
Bad times don't last
The good times go too fast
So as I tumble along
I understand my path isn't aimless now
I'm on the right path
So as you read this book
Enjoy the journey
It will take you through an array of emotions,
feelings, thoughts, and concerns
Know you're not alone
Enjoy!

Fork in the Road

Fork in the road
Left or right
Right or left
A decision needs to be made
The wrong road
should be avoided at all costs
or the happiness regarding life
will just fade away
May the Lord guide you, you ask
but you can't seem to hear Him
Tears roll down your cheeks as you're stuck
and a decision needs to be made
Your intuition
which you always counted on
all of a sudden can't count
The tuition of the road you pick
needs to be paid
And in this school
there is no transferring
Your decision is final
I know it might seem a little extreme
but some decisions are
Some decisions
change your life forever
some for better
and some for worse
in this marriage
you have with life
when you hit the fork in the road

COMMITMENT

Where do my commitment issues come from?
My commitment issues
started from past commitments
that had issues
from communication
loyalty, love, and trust that were misused
What you don't know can't hurt
But once you know
you're confused
You don't really feel pain at first
still trying to process the betrayal
They say time heals all wounds
but some wounds are too deep
And instead of dying physically
you die emotionally
Unfortunately,
if you pull that knife out
you would bleed out
So it stays lodged inside you
As time passes the scar tissue
accepts the knife and it becomes a part of you
So the emotional things become hard to do
and physical things become easy
So I can build a house
but living in it
makes me apprehensive
I'm a wounded soldier

My partner once set me up
Left me to die
sent me to my demise
in order to gain
So even on the sunniest day
I think of rain and the pain
The train wreck
I barely survived
So I focus my energy on becoming the ultimate soldier
Too physically strong to fall
too mentally strong to fail
Because if I show weakness
I could die
So you see why I run away from commitment
I almost bled out once
So to attempt to commit to her
I have to remove this knife
allow myself to be vulnerable
and hope she will nurse me back to health
never misusing my wounded heart

DATE

The fire once burned bright
through the day and night
through the rain and wind
It flickered here and there
through those rough times
but always remained strong
It was born to burn bright
regardless of the elements
stronger than the Hulk, Superman, and Iron Man combined
After years and years of fighting and winning
the most uneven of fights
this fire grew hotter in its core
and brighter to the naked eye
So determined to outlast all the elements thrown at it
to one day be strong and big enough
to warm the world
There was a storm approaching
that was going to be challenging
But the fire was so strong and determined
it wasn't even worried
But this storm wasn't like any other storm
it had ever seen before
The fire shined with a certain flare
as the storm passes laughing at it
not knowing everything has an expiration date
And that night when it shined as bright as ever
happened to be his date with fate
his date with darkness

WEATHER

I tried to fight it for years
Changing people's minds
Turning tears to smiles
frowns upside down
But all it ended up doing
was bringing me down
surrounding me with black clouds
when all I wanted were those hot sunrays
So now I'm done
learned my lesson
Wish it had occurred in less time
Now I read energy
if they bring rain and pain
I maneuver as fast as possible away
Because
if they can't see the beauty in life
those black clouds
will always be their forecast
My weather needs to be sunny
My storms have passed
and I refuse to live in the past
So now it is time
to soak up my sunrays
not the rain anymore

Just Know

Honestly
you've got to stop
thinking off the top
that these other women got a shot
Trust is a must
They don't compare to you
So I can't love them
No interest
Can't touch them
No interest
Can't hold them down
No interest
Simply because they aren't you
So know I might not always say it
but I need a bigger word than love
to express my feelings for you
Just so you know
from this day forward
I devote myself to you
There will be no need to question
You got to understand, baby
You're my queen
I live to keep a smile on your face
I live to keep you safe
I live to keep you falling in love with me
each and every day

Sleepless Nights

I lay down wide awake
wondering
why, when, where, what is happening
I look at the younger version of myself
And I'm perplexed
on when my train
went off the rails
My life isn't anything like
I planned it to be
It's moving at a snail's pace
without a trace
Feel so out of place
Trying to figure out where
I made that crucial mistake
that got me feeling this disgrace
I'm supposed to have it all by now
I'm supposed to have figured it all out by now
But this Rubik's cube of life
is a lot harder than expected

A Letter to My Father (Part 1)

I had to grow up without you
because you were too stubborn
to accept being governed
So, I had to suffer
Not because my mother wasn't there
But because you didn't care enough to be
Had to see other kids with their dads on Fathers' Day
Handing them the cards they made
My card never went to you
because I didn't know where you stayed
It always went to that woman
you forced to play two main roles
She had to throw the ball around with me
Teach me how to be tough enough to be able to survive
in this cold world
Sweet enough to one day
make a girl my world
Driven enough to feel I could be
the President of the United States
before there was an Obama
Respectful enough to be loved
and cherished by grandma
She had to kill some of her dreams
so my dreams could be born
We became a team

I had her back
and she had mine
At least
that's what I believed
Me being so young
how could I really have her back
But I knew you didn't have mine
I resented you and my name
because we shared it
My mother
has never called me by that name though
I told her I wanted to change it
She said I couldn't until I was eighteen
which meant I had a long way to go
Fast-forward
now I'm eighteen
and ready to change my whole name
I tell her it's time
for me to take her last name not have yours
She tells me
"Thank you, but I don't need that"
I couldn't believe it
She had the opportunity
to support me
and get rid of you for good
and said no
Months after I realized why
she didn't want me to change it
She wanted me to accept it
and be better because of it
I promised myself I wouldn't be like you
Yes
I share your name
your DNA
some of your features
but not the heart and the ability to leave

my future kid behind
That's the day
I realized
I was already a better man
than you ever were
Every Father's Day
I say "Happy Father's Day"
to my mom proudly
So, I say "thank you"
for the only lesson you taught me
unintentionally
to be nothing like you

LOVE

Live life to the fullest because it's short
Open your heart to new possibilities
Value yourself always
Everything, even heartache is worth experiencing
Love even if it's just once

FISHERMAN

Some girls love the pain
they can cause
How weak and lost they can have a man
How she can suck the life out of you
slowly
drop by drop
where your concerns
are only her concerns
and her concerns never benefit you
But you don't see it or care to
She's your drug
Your friends and family warn you
over and over
but you're hooked
deeper than a fish
on a fisherman's hook
So, you will go
where she leads you
until she gets bored enough
and leaves you out to dry
Drugs come in different forms
Don't be the next one
on a fisherman's hook

LOVE?

I don't know
what real love is like
or if it even exists
The truth is
all I know is the pain it brings
Once I think I've met someone
who can change my mind
it ends up being another fling
I resist the thought that maybe
I was meant to be alone
Because
how can I be a king
and have my throne without a queen
The thought alone is unclean
I just pray one day
God will intervene
and bring love to me
So the dream comes to be reality
and love can finally have its eulogy

DECISIONS

I made a very tough decision
Since then it's been uneasy
how I've been feeling
debating
if this alternate route I'm on, full of doubt
will pan out
Or will I get lost
and lose my mind in the process
My life is a mess
I'm stressed
and lost the ability to decompress
I've been told you need to hit rock bottom
to be able to grow
Either I made the right decision
or the wrong one
But at least
I can hang my head on the fact that
I made a decision
Please know
I did what I thought was best for us

LOSS FOR WORDS

...
Don't know what to say
I used to say
I could never live without you
And you know it was true
So you mistreated me
and didn't care
But now those thoughts have gone astray
Your hold on me has lost its grip
Don't trip though
We had our run
We had our fun
Had amazing times together
Key word is *had*
because I'm leaving you in the past at last
Nothing else left to say
but goodbye

Knock, Knock

We had it all
and I messed it up and now
I'm here knocking on your door
With thirty-six long-stemmed roses in my hand
I've been gone for a good while
Been doing my own thing
Enjoying the freedom
I have this whole speech ready for you
hoping you open that door
Knock, knock
I just hope I remember my spiel
How I thought
I could do it on my own
And I did for a while
Grew up a lot though
This journey without you is lonely
and not worth taking
Just hope you're still single
We belong together
The problem is you knew it from the beginning
and I'm just realizing it now
I hope I'm not too late
and that ship hasn't sailed
it's still at the docks
I just want to say I love you
and can I have the honor
of being the last man
you will ever have
Door opens

Supposed To

I'm supposed to
spend the rest of my life with you
But being with you
doesn't allow rest
It's a mess
with a shitload of stress
It's impressive
that I've made it this far
I want to leave her
but every time I try
the pain is too much to bear
So I keep running back
She knows
I won't ever leave her
And that drives me crazy
It's amazing
a free man
but a slave to her
since the day we met

FEELINGS

Tell me
why I don't have any
Tell me
why I feel better alone
most of the time
Why my mind works
differently than most
Well, all
Haven't met anyone
quite like myself
I definitely know
that's a good thing though
How can I be so social
But rather be anti
Why is it that people
have never given me the feeling
music and sports have
How I see the most light in the dark
How darkness to me is an opportunity
How I want to be able to feel again
Want someone to get me
Be the missing piece of my jigsaw puzzle

ME

Who is he?
That's a good question
Let me answer that for you
On one side
he is a professional basketball player
who has spent more time on the bench
in street clothes than with his uniform on
The last time he played without an injury
he was a senior in high school
who's had some of the best
and the worst coaches
throughout his career
A man
who has thought of quitting
or retiring a million times
due to the toll taken on by his body, mind,
and the lack of success
A man who is emotionally
physically and mentally unstable
Who has consistent fights
with the Man above
because he's not where he thinks he should be
With some skeletons in his closet
Some regrets in his back pocket
A hole where his loving heart used to be
Covered in scars from head to toe
some visible and some unseen
by the naked eye

A man
who is very selfish at times
Sometimes unreasonable
Who has been with a lot of women
Sees love as a fairy tale
Who has taken advantage of them
Who has cheated on some
lied to others
And the lucky ones
got the combo package
Easily loses interest
and hardly amused
A man
who is antisocial
doesn't like letting people
get too close to him
Who at times can't stand that
others are succeeding more than him
Someone who doesn't forgive as often as he should
Who is self-centered at times
Wears his headphones so loud that
he doesn't have to hear the real world
or talk to people like that
On the flip side
who is he?
He is
a man of principle
A man
who is big on honesty
A man
who believes in loyalty
Wants to believe in love
A man
that adapts to the situations

presented to him
Who turns negatives into positives
in one way or the other
Who isn't a quitter
A man
who cares way too much
A man
that doesn't judge
who is always there for the people
he cares about
or even someone he just met
Someone
always willing to help anyone
that could use the help or advice
Good at reading people
Easily entertained
A man
who sees the world
and sees a million possibilities
A man
who knows he will be great one day
and will bring positive change to the world
A family man
whose heart is made of gold
when it comes to them
A man
with two degrees
A man
that has been counted out
every turn along the way
and always finds a way
of being added in
when it's all said and done
Someone

who is used to fighting an uphill battle
Someone
who will win
at the end of the day
A man
who has grown and learned
from his mistakes
Who has dreams of having a family of his own
and becoming the best father
and husband possible
A man
who has high aspirations for himself
publishes a poetry book like his father did
even though he doesn't talk or see him
A man
who strives to be a better person every day

LOSING BATTLE

It's funny how
what I've given my life to
has limited my ability to live life.
It's funny how
I have pursued her
with my all my might
and she pushes me away
but keeps me close enough
that I can't stay away.
It's funny how
my addiction feeds my soul
and makes me happy
like nothing else
but it's killing my body
every day more and more.
But if I die anytime soon,
it will be giving my life to you,
pursuing you,
being addicted to you.
Why?
Because
I hope for that day
that you realize
I was the one,
you should've given your life to,
the one that you should've ran to,
the one
who you should've been addicted to as well.
But until that day,
I'm in a losing battle…

FIGHT

Life is beautiful
Our similarities
and differences
as individuals
make us unique and amazing
to say the least
Some individuals think
that by causing pain and suffering
they will get their point across
They will bring fear to the hearts
of beautiful people and keep them
from spreading love and happiness
My gift to the people
spreading hate
is that I will spread
more love
I will smile more
and show them regardless of what they do
they won't make this life
not worth living for me

SUICIDAL THOUGHTS

Thoughts of suicide
have crept into my mind
on how
I can just swallow
a handful of pills
and let go
Be free
Even had the pills in my hand
a couple of times
But then
I think about my family
my mom
It's not the natural order of things
for a mother
to have to bury her child
Then I think about
my sister and brother
and all I've told them about life
and working hard
How life isn't easy
but it's beautiful
How can I say that but then
do such a selfish, ugly thing?
So, my suicidal thoughts
will stay a mere fantasy of freedom
until I find a way to free myself
from my troubles

PAIN

Something
I endure every day
In various ways
Hours
I feel without pain
Seem strange
My body and mind
aren't on the same page
Most of the time
in different books practically
Looks can be deceiving
My smile hides the pain
I have inside
Most of my pain is physical
but this toll on the bridge
to my brain
is becoming too expensive to pay
I've tried different things
to get the easy pass
away from this traffic jam of pain
One
two
three
four
fuck, these pills
aren't working anymore
How many can I take
before this easy pass
becomes the reason I pass?

IN LOVE

I'm in love with this girl
She rocks my world
No other girl
has even come close
No wonder
it didn't work with anyone else before
God had been getting me ready for the day
when I met her
From the moment
I saw her
I would see her true worth
Knew she would be the one
to change the way
I've been living
from driving in the fast lane
to driving on the shoulder
because
I want to be able to
appreciate every moment with her
so I can cherish, love, and adore her
like no other
I want the entire world to know
I love her
yet I've never met her
she's the woman of my dreams
that no woman
I've met has ever been able to live up to
So, either I'm going to be single forever
or God is going to come through with you

Butterflies

I remembered
when I finally got the courage to say hello
Before that
I'd just look at you from afar
admiring your beauty
Truly had no idea
that admiration
would turn into love
A love that's lasted over a decade
and every time
I'm with you
I feel butterflies
like the first time
I met you

Mind My Business

Growing up I learned to always
mind my business
and the world would be a place
to consider stress-free-ish
But I'm finding it hard to
mind my business
when my mind is always on business
And for these extra hours
it keeps me up at night
I don't get paid for
I strive for greatness
and have encountered tons of pain
Enough to make me gain
a new perspective on life
but I refuse to fall
when I was built to stand tall
Sometimes times are hard
but it's better to have tough times
than no time at all
I'm saying it's better to
eat stale bread than eat nothing at all
So, I'm going to tell my mind
tonight to take a break
and instead of counting
sheep and troubles
till I pass out
I'll count my blessings and successes
praying for more in the future

PULLED OVER

My eyes get watery
as I realize
I might be
making some eyes water
I might not see my daughter again
as the officer approaches me
the news hits
the media channels
that a young man
covered in red
is lying dead
on the pavement
A car ride
gone wrong
And the thought of that
kills me
License and Registration

STUCK

The way I feel about her
is kind of comical
Is it possible
I tried to have her subliminally
through all the relationships I've had
If that's the case
its kind of sad
If I look back
every girl I dealt with
looks like her
Maybe I should call her
and see why
I keep all these thoughts of her
Maybe
I can give them back
and get myself back on track

IDK

I used to think love
was a beautiful thing
But isn't love an addiction?
Depicted in delusional ways
With a lot of laughs
hugs
kisses
good wishes
and other beautiful things
When the truth of the matter is
love is like a hurricane
inside the eye
you're fine
but everything outside of it
is ruined
Outside the eye
is the addiction part of love
not depicted
the heartbreak
depression
the pain

SCARED

I could say
I'm not scared of anything
But why lie?
Everyone has fears
some small
some big
some tall
like a wall
keeping you away from reaching
your full potential
Crippling you from
flying like you
were meant to
Instead you're caged
and since this is the first time
we are meeting
I think it's better to
start off our relationship
with no lies
I am scared
but I won't let fear
guide my path any longer
keeping me away from my potential
I don't know
what to expect
going down this road
But I'm ready
to face my fears
to turn my current fears
into old memories

PERSEVERANCE

Life is a battlefield
that will rattle you to the core
Leave you wounded
and hurt for sure
Make living another day
sometimes a chore
At times will make you
feel like a whore
Used, dirty, and unworthy
Sometimes the story
looks gloomy and blue
As you see the world's
your friends', your families' issues
on top of your own
In the battlefield
you hold your gun
shooting
trying to get out of this mess
Soldiers fall to the right and left of you
Making you wonder
Should I just keep fighting?
Everyone around me is dying
Is my fate already sealed?
But you've got to keep fighting
keep moving forward
in order to succeed
Wounds heal

and leave scars on your canvas
to remind you of your past struggles
and current growth
Glad you've persevered
and now you can appreciate
how far you have come

HER

The first time I met her
she changed my view
I knew we had to be together
I wanted to get to know, the real her
No one-night stand
Didn't want her to be
my summer honey
or winter bunny
Wanted it to last forever
like my money
I knew if I got her
it would be forever
Had to show her
I would treat her better
than others have in her past
That this kind of love
would last a lifetime or two
The kind of life the two of us can have
would make the happiest couple sad
all types of mad
The more I've gotten to know you
the more in love I fall
All the guys want you
all the girls are jealous of you
but you're mine
You make it clear you only need me
and I show you daily
how my eyes are only for you

But regardless of the hate
our fate is sealed by love
ruled by us
I promise to honor you
love you
lust you
trust you
You are my queen
I am your king
Together possibilities are endless
Without you my life would be a mess
So until the day I die
Every single day and night
My promise will be kept

FATHERLESS

Fatherless beginnings
made me bitter and sad
Mad at everyone
who had their dad
What did I do
that was so bad
that you're gone
I blamed myself for so long
But I was young,
stupid, and wrong
just longing for your approval
At times it was just brutal
But then it hit me
at about the age of sixteen
That I would be a better man
than he
Because she
my mother
raised me to be
And because of that fact
the fatherless son
becomes a father
and fathers his son
The trend that could have started
never becomes

Cheating

Is there ever a time
when a person's reason for cheating
can sound so strong
not to be considered wrong?
Or is it just wrong
regardless of the song
they depict to play?
She lies in the arms of another man
Her man
Damn, if he only knew
when she says she
has to stay late at work
the only work she's doing
I would consider cruel
She comes home after
Without a thought of shame
Her man
hears the keys jingling
Can't wait to kiss her face
Not knowing it was just below
the waist of another
Can't wait to hold her
Not knowing
she was being held by another
It's sad
but happens all the time
people living a double life

True Colors

They say animals
see in black and white
It's sad
that they're at a disadvantage
while we see in color
Everyone loves color
and all the shades
But how many times
have you uttered the words
I didn't see his or her true colors
Too many times to count, I know
People are either too naive or gullible
enclosed behind a wall
or enslaved by scars
left behind by the one who swore to the heaven skies
they would never do you wrong
It's the same old song
But if people saw in
black and white only
we would go through less pain
wouldn't turn so many sunny days into rainy ones
The more color
the more shades
The more shades
the harder it becomes
to figure out people's true colors
I guess we are really the ones
who are at a disadvantage
not the animals after all

ADDICTION

My name is _____
and I am an addict
I'm here today
to express to you
the trials and tribulations
I go through with my addiction
Most nights
I don't sleep
just because
I'm thinking of my next fix
I know
I'm sick
so I'm here for help
Because I wonder if the world
would even know if I was gone
What have I done wrong?
How did this addiction
take complete control over me?
Will it ever let go of me?
I try to find a drug to substitute it,
but nothing works
At times
I think it's a punishment
a curse
That made me a puppet
a pet to my addiction
In addition
I have no one to talk to about it

Because I feel embarrassed
and start getting depressed
when I think about the prison
I've put myself into
But I'm here trying to be strong
Stronger than I've ever been
I dream of a day
where my addiction
and I can be together in harmony
But addiction and harmony
sit on opposite sides of the balance beam
when it comes to me
So until I figure out how to live without it
I'll be a prisoner without bars to it
Nothing is worse

Saying Goodbye

This is one of the hardest things
I know I have to do
I've always chosen you
before everything and everyone
But I have to say goodbye to you
It's time
the pain
sleepless nights
and the tears shed over the years
have taken a toll on me
This bill
has become too expensive
for me to pay any longer
But let me say this
I love you dearly
and always will
You did so much for me
I dreamt of a life
where we were joined at the hip
But you had different plans
You didn't want me
And you did everything to break us up
And I did everything
to keep us together
But you win
I'm done
Goodbye
I can't fight anymore
My spirit is broken

WHY

You make my mind wonder first
And slowly you choke me
But I can still breathe pretty normal
Then you get mad at me
and start applying more pressure
I tell you to stop
I can't breathe
and you just choke me harder
Seeing my life start to flash right before my eyes
Because it doesn't matter what I do
those hands are too strong for me to remove
I'm sorry for whatever I did
Just let me go
But your mission is the death of me
Slowly my eyes roll back
and I can't fight for air anymore
I just leave my fate in your hands
and you decide to hand me off to death
as I say goodbye

Still Remember

I still remember
the first time I saw you
Went over to see my best friend
and there you were
sitting on the couch
with that long hair
pretty face, juicy lips, and that smile
Looking like a piece of heaven on earth
Everything just clicked for me
I became more addicted
with every word she spoke
I felt like a kid in a candy store
Knew she had to be my girl
Unfortunately
I had set prior plans
and had to leave her
She started getting ready to go out
and hopped in the shower
I told my best friend
I needed her
She said, "I knew you guys would hit it off"
Can't stall anymore
I have to leave my ride's outside waiting
blowing up my phone
when all I want to do is postpone my exit
and see where this unknown chemistry would lead to
for her and me so
I knock on the door

So I can get a simple hug and tower over her
and make her feel safer
than she ever has in her life in anyone's arms
She said, "You can't come in
I'm naked, doing my makeup"
"It's nothing I haven't seen before
come give me hug before I go" I replied
"I'm not going to open the door" she continued
"So, I will do the honors then" I replied
and silence came from the other side of the door
Opened the door slowly
and my eyes couldn't believe the sight they had
I was completely unaware
of how much deeper I could fall for her
when I just met her earlier
My eyes were glued on her
as I scanned her from head to toe
and she just looked at me
then continued doing her makeup
At that point I promised myself
that this would be the first and last time
I saw her like that
and couldn't have my way with her
my queen-to-be

WHO?

Who are you?
I don't even recognize you anymore
You used to be my lady
All my future plans had you in them
I was supposed to grow old with you
But those days
seem like a distant memory
You changed
and not for the better
Estranged
How did this happen?
Did you put on a show
the whole time we were together
like you were onstage?
Did this happen to maintain yourself
when you and I ended?
Or did it happen with age?
Did you feel caged?
I wanted to proclaim my love for you
for the world to see
Get engaged, married
But I would have made a big mistake
Ashamed by my poor judgment
Guess I just have to accept the fact
that girl I knew
doesn't exist anymore
and probably never did

My Father's Child

My father and I
are very alike
We love sports
love being right
and telling people
"I told you so"
Also love to prove people wrong
Have to have a good woman by our side
He worked at CBS
I worked at CNN
He wrote a poetry book
Here I am publishing mine
He ran the NYC marathon
And I just ran my first NYC marathon
I was nervous and excited at the same time
When I crossed that finish line
my father wasn't there though
to hug me, to cry with me, laugh, or compare medals with
Not because he died
but because he's never been a father to his child
But our paths in life overlap decades apart
So even though he never fathered me
I can't deny the fact that I'm his child

Man's Best Friend

Bruce
thank you for the memories
relentless love
understanding how I was feeling
the chance to be your best friend
Eternally grateful
I love you
and I miss you dearly
Until we meet again

CAN'T BE

I checked my phone
Expecting a message
from this little cutie
I've been talking to
But it's not her
Unfortunately
it's one of my boys
telling me that you got arrested
and being charged with murder
I can't believe it
thought it was a joke
But no, it's true
Someone isn't alive
and you're the person of interest
I can't fathom you doing this
So, I impatiently wait for the real facts to come out
All these different versions
affect me deeper and deeper
You were my brother
even though
we didn't chill like that
even though
we spoke sparingly
Between us
it's always been love
A lot of talking wasn't needed
We spoke about linking up
And now you're chained up

Not the type of links
we spoke about though
Now for me to see you
I'm going to have to see you in court
from a distance
or talking through a phone
with that glass between us
I have so many questions
I want to ask you
that burn inside me
Your life has changed forever
Mine has been affected forever
If you did it, I hate what you did
feel disgusted, disappointed by it
But who am I to judge
I'mma keep the love
I have for you
And I'll ask God
to take care of you, your family, and hers

30

I'm about to be
thirty years old
What if I told you
I never thought
I would see 21
    22
    23
    24
    25
    26
    27
    28
    29
Now
I'm a couple of days
shy of being thirty
Almost died three times
I might have nine lives
but I can't live any other way
than like I might not see 31

Mommy

I can't write a poem about you
the way I would love to
Because
I can't think of the perfect sequence of words
to describe
how vital you've been in my life
I love you
and
I'm sorry because of that

THE GAME

She met this guy
She thought it would be fun to fuck with
He was tall, dark, and handsome
who had a smile
that could make the saddest person
crack a smile
His personality and unpredictable way
of being and thinking
cracked that bolted door
Fuck
he figured her out
She would wake up
and go to sleep thinking of him
It wasn't all fun and games anymore
because she had fallen
without even realizing
They were both neck-deep in it
afloat due to a log
Happy at least
or so he thought
She was looking for a way out
because she was sure
he would leave her
there to drown soon enough
So, one day a lifeboat
with a familiar face drove by
and she got on
while he slept

He woke up
and she was gone
thinking she might have drowned
in his sleep
Without knowing how to swim
he let the log go
and down he went looking for her
Knowing by doing that
his fate was sealed
The chance of finding her
and giving her one last kiss
before the lights went out
was worth it to him
If only he knew
she went with another
because she was afraid
one day he would leave her
Not knowing
he was willing to die for her
The games we play

Behind Closed Doors

She lives a double life
And no
she's not a superhero
What she does though is
somewhat heroically unnoticeable
And no
she's not cheating on anyone
besides herself daily
And no
she's not a criminal
well in the sense
of being looked for by law enforcement
But she's behind bars
She smiles daily to balance
the tears she shed the night before
makes sure everyone around her is well
But no one checks on her well-being ever
They assume she's good
because she appears strong
And the more she deteriorates
the more helpful she becomes
As she cries herself
to sleep every night
longing for someone
to give her a reason to smile
The acting job she does
should be looked at by the academy
As she gets older

it's getting worse and worse
She comes up to a fork in the road
And this decision
will decide her fate
can she keep the act up
or garner the strength to stand up
and say no more
that role isn't for me anymore
or will she allow the director to kill her off
because the show would be better without her
I just hope she didn't choose
a Robin Williams fate
Haven't heard from her
in a couple of days

TEXT

I got a text
"Hey, I really need to talk you," he said
"What's going on?" I replied
"It's not an emergency
but the sooner we can talk about it the better," he continued
"All right, I'll let you know
when I'm back around my way," I replied
"Bet"
All day I wondered what it could be
Figured he got into some drama
messing with some girl
that he shouldn't have been with
and her man found out
Maybe his mom kicked him out again
and he needs a place to crash
or he's in love for the thousandth time
with a new girl he met like yesterday
When I got back
I texted him back
"Bruh, I'm around
let me know when you wanna get up?"
He said, "Now"
Caught me off guard
but I said, "ight cool, where you wanna meet?"
"Let's go to the courts," he said
I got a ball, let's get some shots up, it's been a while
When I got there
he's already there getting shots up
"What's good, bruh?

What's going on?
You scaring me
Who you got pregnant?" laughing, I asked
He said, "Let's get some shots up first
then we'll talk about what's going on later"
We got a workout in like back in the days, felt good
About an hour into the workout
he blurred out, "I'm gay"
I just kept shooting
He yelled out, "Bruh, I'm gay!"
And I replied, "Okay"
He stopped rebounding
and said, "I'm serious
I'm gay
I like men"
I was like, "Okayyyyyy"
Then he said, "I came out to my family
and they called me a slur of names
and kicked me out
I'm coming to you
because you're my dude
not like that, you know what I mean
I can't live a lie anymore
I needed to be honest with myself
been hiding it over ten years
couldn't do it a day longer"
As tears started rolling down his face
I just stared at him
with a blank facial expression
And he looked at me
desperate for me to say something
"Say something, please"
Then I replied to him
"I don't know
what is appropriate to say or not

Obviously
this isn't where I thought the conversation was going to go
So, you're gay
like gay gay
kissing-guys gay
not like you're happy, gay?"
He said, "Yes, I'm gay
I like guys"
I replied with a smirk
"So this means you are going to have
a lot of single female friends to introduce me to"
He looked up with a shocked look
"Listen," I continued
"Proud of you for coming out
Obviously, I'm not gay but you my dude
we have always had each other's back for years now
Now everything I say sounds gay
Ha ha ha, look what you have done
Nothing is going to change between us, bruh
You're like a brother
Just now you're my gay brother"
He hugged me and said, "Thank you
I thought of killing myself today
Thanks to you
I'm thinking about all the new possibilities of life
It will be hard
but I'm going to fight
and make it work"
You never know how important
you are to someone.
You never know what someone is going through
What demons they battle on the daily
Let's be more understanding,
more loving, and less judgmental.

THANK GOD FOR ~~TRAGEDY~~

Is it bad that
I'm grateful for the world's tragedies?
Why would I say some shit like that?
How could I even think that travesty?
Some of you might stop reading this now
How can I be grateful for earthquakes
hurricanes, tsunamis, floods, premature deaths
etc., etc., etc.?
Instead of asking me how
better question is…
Why does it take one of these things to happen for us to wake up
and put all the nonsense aside?
When you're at risk of losing your life
it doesn't matter if you're a cop
doesn't matter if you're Black, Latino, White
etc., etc.
It doesn't matter if you're an immigrant
or born here
It doesn't matter if you're tall,
short, fat, skinny, or muscle bound
If your complexion is as white as snow
or as dark as coal
and all the shades in between
Doesn't matter if you're a Republican or Democrat
None of those things matter
But unfortunately
it takes one of these events to occur
for us to realize we all need each other

We all are beautiful
We all are people
We all have families and feelings
So, until we realize this
on a day-to-day basis
and we eliminate the hate
that so many live with daily
tragedies will be the only thing
to bring us together
So, I thank God for them
Unfortunately

God, I Got Some Questions

God
you're the Almighty
But I talk to you
like you're one of my boys
Because that's the kind of relationship we have
Some don't like it but who cares
You accept me for me
and I appreciate
all you have done for me
and my family
I know you're busy
But I have some questions
Maybe you can lead me to the answers
or even answer them for me, yourself
Why are innocent babies
sometimes born with disabilities
or meant not to survive long or at all?
Why did you make us
in so many beautiful shades
yet there are people
who hate us for our color?
Why does your house close
During the hours the devil is out and about the most?

Family Feuds

Families
are supposed to be the highest form
of compassion, happiness, support
strength, loyalty, love, trust
and togetherness you can find
But the reality is
it's not the highest form
of most of these things I've mentioned
So behind closed doors
we fight, argue, cry
ignore, avoid, enable each other
But when the doors open
you would think
we were the Brady Bunch
Something about it being publicized
that your family isn't perfect
That scares the toughest man or woman
So, we live in an alternate reality
but this isn't *Stranger Things*
and on this side
the alternate world
is just a rug over dust and dirt
you aren't ready to expose
Come to grips with
and attempt to clean up
But know no one's family is perfect
some members are selfish
some are cheap

some are manipulators
some are jealous
among other things
But let's not forget some are amazing
some are supportive,
compassionate, loving, loyal, trustworthy
and the main reason
you are the wonderful person you are today
And some family members
aren't even blood relatives
Just know family feuds happen
to all families
rich and poor
big and small

Mine

I'm about to take you there
a place you've never been before
In this place
your body doesn't belong to you anymore
In this place
you have no say
In this place
every inch of your body
will be under my control
Every feeling you feel
will be controlled by me
I'mma tie you up first
Start with your arms
then your legs
each to a corner of the bed
Blindfold you
put some music on
Really low
I want all your senses
to be on high alert
as I plan on taking my time
first disconnecting your mind
from reality
In this place
where pleasure reigns
accompanied by some pain
As I make you mine

Thoughts of the Dead

People
reading my thoughts
scares me
These poems
are just words from thoughts
that kept me up at night
that weigh heavily on my shoulders
even heavier on my mind
In order to continue living
in this chaotic world
I had to write them down
for two reasons
one being if the cold world starts changing me
I could go back and read this book
and see where it started
and two being
I could revisit a part of me
in these words that
probably no longer exists

BRUCEEEE

I miss you daily
Having you was a blessing
an honor
a privilege
Now you're gone
and I'm not sure
how to get past that
The fact that when I open the door
you're not running towards me
The fact that you won't slightly wake up
and lay on your back so I can rub on your belly
as you go back into a deep sleep
The fact that regardless of
how shitty a day I had
How much I failed
What mistake I made
I always was a hero in your eyes
Always the best
You were always happy to see me
Even at times
when I wasn't happy to see myself
I love you and miss you
Thank you for allowing me
to grow with you
and even though
you're not here physically
you live within me every day
You're the background on my phone

So, I also get to see you every day
I'll remember all the amazing days
We had together
until I get to heaven's doors
and you're the first one to greet me

ENGAGEMENT

She said
she's engaged now
She couldn't believe it
She has gone through a lot
and despite her flaws and scars
someone saw past the damaged goods sign
and got on one knee
And she flaunts that ring
for everyone to see
I mean everyone except him
A guy she met
in the most random of ways
but always brightens her day
With him she forgets her past
all her pain and her scars
Her sign doesn't say anything but amazing
So, when he's around
she turns the diamond ring inward
because the way he engages with her
means more to her
than her engagement ring

DON'T TRUST YOU

I don't trust you
I don't trust myself anymore either
I'm kind of stuck
Just wanna say
"Fuck this shit"
I don't need my heart
I'm going to just leave it at home
in my room
in the safe
I have hidden in my closet
behind all those old clothes
I should've donated years ago
because they are all the same
Every time I meet someone
they do something the last person did
and I can't tell if I caught onto the game
or they're being genuine
They're saying all the right things
They must be up to something
because I've seen this movie before
When I think
I found one worth me moving
those clothes in my closet
and opening that safe
I end up covering the safe more
to be able to handle the pain

DEATH

The only thing
we share is death
Regardless of your race,
ethnicity, religious beliefs, political beliefs
sexual preference, musical preference
how many zeros in your bank account
how famous you are
The angel of death comes for all
Sometimes his visits are expected
and other times they break you to the core
So live life like you're going to die soon
Tell everyone your true feelings
Don't leave things unsaid
because we hope
after our loved ones are dead and gone
they can hear us
But what if they can't hear a thing?

THAT GIRL

Told myself
I wouldn't mess with anyone at work
then I met you
well, saw you
I knew that was going to change
That girl
That caramel-skinned beauty
with that long hair and those tattoos
That girl with that smile
had me sprung
A couple of weeks
into starting my new job
Next time I see her
I need to get her number
I saw her two more times
in the most inopportune moments
Didn't get a chance to say much
except wave and say hi
But I promised myself
I would shoot my shot next time I saw her
regardless of what was going on
But that promise
was made a while ago
and I haven't seen her since
Wonder what could've been

COUNTLESS

Baby girl, I know
countless men
have let you down
Countless men
told you they were different
And you believed them
And countless times
you felt stupid and ashamed
They promised you the world
so you gave them your heart
And they returned it back broken
And countless times
you had to put the pieces back together
But like shattered glass
it's never the same again
It has forever changed
And that glass heart
gets more misshapen
With every letdown
In the process changing you

Love Yourself

Is it easier for us to identify our flaws
Easier for us to be consumed by them
Easier for us to find things
we don't love about ourselves
Easier for us to go under a knife
Easier for us to get into a relationship
with all kinds of drugs
Easier for us to quit
Easier for us to commit to suicide
than it is for us to commit to loving ourselves
We have countless blessings
We are all perfectly flawed
Because perfection is boring
Our flaws make us unique
Unlike anyone else
and instead of looking at it like a curse
address it as a blessing
and be grateful
And never forget your worth
Never forget
that we all feel low at times
But never fall out of love with yourself

OCEAN FLOOR

We as humans
are broken, jaded deep inside
You couldn't tell
by looking at the ocean
Because few are willing
to let others dive into their ocean floor
in fear of judgments
As they see all remnants
of the war, battles, pain and mistakes
that can't be erased
from the ocean floor
Would he or she stay
after I let them see the true me?
Through the depth of the ocean floor
can someone see all that
and still want to be with me?
open to removing some of the debris
and set me free

GOD

I just want to say
"Thank you"
because the good in my life
was constructed by you
Sometimes I have to make do
with my current situation
due to the fact
your plans for me
are so far advanced
and better for me
than I can ever see
So I'm writing you
this personal letter
to let you know
I apologize for my shortcomings
and I'm grateful
for your continuous forgiveness
as I strive tomorrow
to be better
than I was today

SUICIDE

I used to think
That suicide
was one of the most horrific things
a human being could do
Now I think it's freeing
to be able to tell your body
mind and troubles
Fuck you, I'm leaving
We are always taught
to forget about public perception
who's going to hate you
not like you
Do what makes you happy
Exception
Is when you want to take your life

THE CALL

I got a call
that you had a stroke
I couldn't believe it
Thought you had passed away
the way the conversation had started
But I was given a chance to see you
and be a good nephew for once
I'm sorry
But it doesn't change anything
I guess even that is selfish
because it allowed me to feel a bit better
But the moment I saw you in that hospital bed
I didn't recognize you
That couldn't be you
But I would know it was you
if I visited more
Dropped by all those times
I said I would
Or called to check on you
Or picked up the phone when you called
or my mom called you
Instead I avoided the calls
because I was watching a movie,
a show, playing video games
or on the phone with the girl of the moment
I had to recheck the room number
and name on the door
And it was definitely you

and you definitely knew who I was
but didn't remember my name
which brought tears to my eyes
Seeing you like that
But I couldn't cry
I'm not allowed to
when I haven't been there
Seeing you struggling to speak
broke my heart
We spoke for hours
and I had no idea
what you were really trying to say
But one of the few
clear things you said
was "I love you"
That broke me even more
How can you love me?
When I haven't been as good
as I should've been to you
because I was upset about something
that happened a decade earlier
But I'm sorry for everything
And I pray every day
you get healthier
and I can make up for lost time
one day at a time

My Mother

Obviously
the most important person in the world
Thank her for all the good
you see in me
and curse the world for all the bad
Her support and love throughout my life
has made me the man I am today
With words like extraordinary, exceptional, and one of a kind
Justice isn't served
in describing her worth
Regardless of whatever I do
she's the only person
that's always in my corner
and for that she deserves the world
And the world I will give her

Fatherhood

I must be changing
because I'm looking at life
a lot differently now
I'm planning things for kids
I haven't had
So I could be the good type of dad
I never had
I want to drown my kids in affection
love and admiration

Unlock

Our loved ones die
And we ask ourselves
several questions starting with "Why?"
Followed by "Why them and not I?
What have I done to deserve this?"
So we lock up our loved ones in a memory box
Too painful to open
So it peeks through every so often
And the pain creeps back out
like it happened yesterday
But what if we opened the box up
embracing our loved ones
Our physical form has limitations
The soul has none
If we tune out the world's noise
we can hear them talking to us
guiding us
What if we realized how blessed we were
to experience that person?
and how their life now lives through us on a daily
The world knows who you are
but might not know about
the amazing person
that contributed to everything you are
So thank that person
Share their story
And remember, legends never die
They inspire

STRINGS

Baby, you don't need me
because I'm really no good
And I've made that clear
But I played your heartstrings
like they've never been played,
so you stay
Even after knowing you deserve better
You are addicted to that song
I play for you
So you stay
playing that broken record on repeat
Even after I told you to get away
and avoid the pain
you stay

You Hate Me

You hate me
because I don't look like you
You hate me
because I don't talk like you
You hate me
because your daughters and sons love us
want to be us
You hate me
because you have done so much to break our spirits
and we continue persevering
You hate me
because you actually think your skin color
means you're better than me
You hate me
because if I move into your neighborhood,
the property value will go down
At least that's the dumb shit you think
You hate me
because through all the negativity and obstacles
created for me to fail
to not succeed, have been unsuccessful
You hate me
because you don't want to understand us
You lump all of us in a group
You hate us
So you kill us like cattle
Your hate sometimes makes us hate ourselves
But that's us no more

You hate us
and call it good police work
You hate us
So you lock us up
You hate us
So we get longer sentences
You hate us
So we live in cages
You hate us
So we live separated from our parents as kids
Because they weren't born here
You hate us
So you do everything possible to break us
But just know
Hate us all you want
We're gonna continue to fight
because letting you win isn't allowed
there's nothing we can't handle
you have done it all and we're still here
because positivity trumps negativity
at the end of the day
the devil might win a battle
but never the war
because fuck you
we are here to stay
And if you have a problem with that
go back to where the fuck you came from
where your great-great-great-grandma and grandpa were born
But just know your hate
tells me I'm great!
tells me I stay on your mind
tells me I'm viewed as a threat
But my value is going up
And no, this time you won't be getting a cut
Those days are long gone

Your Worth

Your worth has been a roller coaster
It goes up and comes down
depending on what's going on in your life
who you're dealing with
how good or bad they have treated you
how off your expectations were
how heavy that societal pressure feels on you
In my opinion
your worth isn't established by anyone
But you
you're gold; your value
always remains the same
whether you have been
emotionally, physically, or mentally
taken advantage of
You decide if you want to carry that baggage forever
or you want to polish up that gold
that whether it's buried or dirty
the value hasn't changed
feel sorry for those
who didn't understand
they had a hand full of gold
and they dropped it.

I Can't Be

I can't be everything you want me to be anymore
The burden's too heavy for me to carry
Your happiness can't depend on me
because I will never really be enough
Even though you think I will
it has to be your own
not owned by me
because I will take care of it at first
But the longer it's in my control
the more likely I am to abuse it
not because I want to but
because my happiness will take priority
At some point
I could marry you
and make your dreams come true
But I don't feel the same way you do
The sun rises and falls with me according to you
In my eyes, the sun rises and falls with or without me
I want to compliment someone
be an added benefit
not your only one
No, this isn't me saying "I'm gone"
It's me saying "I'm done"
I can't be what you want me to be
I hope you understand
that this isn't me removing myself from your life
but me giving you your life back

THANK YOU

Thank you for my troubles
Thank you for my struggles
Thank you for the days I've stumbled
Thank you for the days I've completely crumbled
Sorry for the days I've muddled
cruel words against you
not understanding
I only made it through it
because of you
because you were there
for every step
guiding me through all my mistakes
making every situation
that was overwhelming
somehow manageable
making everything that seemed impossible, possible
making the moments I thought were unbearable, bearable
And now because of all I went through
I look up to the sky
break into prayer
when things go wrong
understanding you're there
always have been and always will be
and because of that fact
I can overcome anything

DON'T FORGET

Don't forget you're beautiful
No, you're not a model
But who said you had to be?
So you might be single
On bumble or tinder swiping
Right or left
And what's wrong with that?
Don't fall victim to societal labels and expectations
They are brutal, cruel, and an unnecessary cycle
we bring to the table
instead of being grateful and thankful for our blessings
So remember, you're beautiful
because you are
and learn to only need validation
from you

What If

What if
we started our day with a smile
instead of a frown
What if
we all listened
instead of talking
What if
we spread positive vibes
instead of negative ones
What if
we looked at everyone as equals
instead of anything less than
What if
doing the right thing was the guide
instead of the bottom line
What if
we admitted our faults and mistakes
instead of making excuses and doubling down
What if
we forgave
instead of holding grudges
How different would the world be
I guess we will never know

CONNECTED

Instead of seeing you, I FaceTime you
Instead of talking to you on the phone, I text you
I like your pictures on Instagram
I send you pictures on Snapchat
comment on your Facebook post
All this technology
all these forms of communication
and we are less connected now
than we were ever before

Not My Fault

How can you be mad at me
I didn't do anything
You came and found me
You were curious
You heard stories
some good
some bad
But you just had to find out for yourself
what I was about
and that's my fault?
You love the fact
that I don't discriminate
in a very tense-filled society
Everyone is welcome to knock on my door
I've been with them all
fat, skinny, ugly, and gorgeous
I get around, but you knew this
I don't pass judgment
So don't judge me
I just make you feel good
I make you feel like you never have before
touch you like your wife wish she could
connect with you in a way your boyfriend
wouldn't understand
I don't talk; I'm just there to listen to you
It's always about you with me
That's why you love me
you fight me

and curse me but you come back
I forgive you for acting crazy
I understand life can be difficult
So now it's just you and me
because your family
friends
and job
don't understand
Our bond
and how unbreakable it really is
Until death, we shall not part
And even after you die,
I'll still be with you for a little while longer
Being me isn't easy
I'm always giving
People are always taking
At the end, I'm always left alone
So why are you mad at me again?

LOVE ME

Love me
Why can't you love me
Why can't you see how much I care for you
how much I've done for you
How can you just disregard that
Not see my beauty
Not see my successes
Not see that I've never left you
and never will
How are you so disgusted by me
When you don't let me do more for you
When you dismiss me
take other people's advice over mine
others' opinions over mine
Love me
Love me
Your reflection in the mirror

Karma

Karma is a bitch
with an itch
to pay you back
for what you have done in this life
good or evil
You will feel it
Either
Karma's loving embrace
or her rejection filled with pain and disgrace

THE BILL

We so often make individuals
who aren't responsible
in charge of taking care of the bill
A bill they didn't rack up
But how many times
has someone hurt you
because they were hurt
they were cheated on
So you are bound to do the same
mentality comes into play
How many times
has someone's past experience
jaded how they have treated you
Allow people to rack up their own bill
Don't have them pay for what your past ordered

SOME

Some people live
Some people die
Some die while they are alive
Some remain alive long after they have died

WANTED

She wanted to be loved
but didn't know how to love
the most important person
in her life: herself

New York, New York

Where dreams come to strive
Where many dreams come to die
A city that, for some, is a jungle
full of hardships and struggles
For others, it's all about the bright lights
status and hustle
Where if you're not mentally strong
you won't survive
because for those born into the jungle
they are wired differently
and that's the only way they survive
But for others who come
based on the allure of the city
fall for the bright lights
end up being eaten up alive
This city will test your
heart, soul, and pride
your loyalty, greed
patience and faith
your morals, love, and hate
Good night's sleep
seem rare and far in between
As the city you call home never sleeps
New York, New York
Welcome, but you've been warned…

Who's Really American

Native American
I think my investigation is complete
Just to educate everyone really quickly
if everyone got sent back to where they came from
this country would be empty
Some had the opportunity to come here hundreds
of years ago and others came yesterday
We all came here with the same goal
same dream
to better our lives
and the lives of our children
America is no one's to claim
And that's why despite
America's ugly past and present
America provides
a hope that's unmatched
Immigrants make this country great
have made it great for ages
Remember you or someone in your family
was once an immigrant
Unless your ancestors
were slaves but that's a discussion
for another day

Burning Bridges

We are conditioned
that under no condition
is it beneficial to burn bridges
But the truth is in order to move on
in order to grow
we must leave and never return
to that place of hurt
that place of pain
that place of belittling
that place of shame
And those burning bridges
give us direction
on where we need to go
how far we have come
So burn some bridges
Light up your sky
Say goodbye to the old you
as you embark on this journey
And say hello to the person you are becoming
It's overdue

THE IRONY

The obsession
we have with things
we don't possess
and the blunt disregard
for the things we do
For a broke man
with a rich heart
money is everything
For a rich man
with a broken heart
money is nothing

Caged Open

I've been through a lot physically
been through a lot emotionally
Have had my faith tested multiple times
Sometimes I failed and sometimes I barely passed
On a few occasions, I passed outright
But instead of asking "Why me?"
for the millionth time, it seems like
I decided to pat myself on the back
For all the challenges I've faced
and somehow overcome, despite
all the physical pain
all the emotional letdowns
and the times my faith was down and out
has allowed me to become the man I am today
A better man because of these struggles
So now I thank God every day for everything I have
And I try to spread that love to others
Because for the first time in a long time
I feel like a cageless bird
I can finally spread my wings
be the real me
and consistently be
happy and free

LIVING DEAD

She went to the party
A girl with a bright future
Optimistic about the world
Full of life, but that all changed
Why did you do it?
Why did you decide to do the shit you did?
Hurt that girl the way you did
Was it because she was hot?
had a fat ass?
big boobs?
Or you heard a rumor that she was easy?
Or were you just horny and she wanted it
According to you?
So you invite her upstairs
You start kissing her
and you force yourself on top of her
start undressing her
she says, "No, please stop"
as you cover her mouth
Because you don't care
She's gonna get that dick
She went upstairs
She knew what that meant
And you deserve it, right?
As you penetrate her
With every stoke
She dies
a little more and more

until she's completely dead
And you take her lack of fighting
as she wants it now
As you finish
she stays there in disbelief
You say that was fun
and you leave
go downstairs to continue partying
celebrating your conquest
while she's contemplating death
in its truest sense
She got dressed
and left that party
A wounded woman
with a future forever haunted by her new past
A world that would forever be hopeless
Behind bars in every sense of the word
Dead inside
and now she's the definition of the living dead
Before you create the next living dead woman
think about the women in your life
who have been able to live their lives
and how different your life would've been
if they had died while living

MONEY

Money is the root of all evil
will turn a friend to a foe
your wifey to a hoe
have your ride or die
set you up
and watch you die in your ride
Money blurs the moral compass of life
makes you feel untouchable
allows you to surround yourself
with everything you dreamed of
Yet you are lonelier than ever
Money won't change you
Just expose the real you

IF YOU KNEW...

If you knew the real me
you probably wouldn't love me
If you knew the real me
you sure as fuck would judge me
If you knew the real me
you would know I've made a ton of mistakes
I've given in to societal pressures
I'm ashamed to say
If you knew the real me
you would know I struggle
to be the man my mom raised me to be
a man of faith, love and integrity
When my faith in humanity
has been shaken to the core
In a world where my skin color is still an issue
Where everyone's life doesn't seem to have the same value
A world where we rather record and post
instead of helping someone in need
My faith in God hasn't broken but definitely has bent
as I ask why, over and over again
in a world where likes are more important than love
Where instant gratification outshines hard work
Where outer appearances mean everything
And your true self, the actual person, means nothing
A world where money buys love
Where kids are considered a business decision, not a blessing
where integrity can be used against you
Where if you don't lose some of those morals

your path of success becomes narrower
because you gotta fit a mold
So every time I find a road that fits me
Feeling like I'm going down the right path
There happens to be another road closure
and I have to take the next exit
take an alternate route
Alternate routes come with alternate thoughts
Alternate thoughts come with alternative actions and reactions
So, I struggle on the daily to be a man of faith, love and integrity
my mom raised me to be
She's proud though; I'm still trying
and will continue to fight against the waves
until my dying day
because letting her down isn't an option
and letting the world win isn't one either

FIGHTING

Fight for your rights
because they won't
Fight for your happiness
because they won't
Fight for your dreams
because they won't
Fight the urge to discount your worth
because they will never want to pay full price
Fight for you
because you're special
because you are literally a 1 of 1
Doesn't get rarer than this
But don't fight for them to see your worth
If they don't see it
or better yet your light frightens them
keep them in fear
Don't stop fighting
Fight more
Don't dim your light to appease anyone's eyes
They shouldn't get to appreciate any of it
So when they say you're not this or that material
when they say you aren't good enough
or they just over look you
it's not your loss
it's theirs
Be grateful and walk away
Some battles are worth fighting
others aren't necessary

you already won
because you chose self-worth
over self-doubt
So your stock will continue to increase

Don't Love Me Like That

Don't love me like that
because I don't know
how to deal with it
The fact that you're everything
I've always wanted
But my past has me jaded
So don't love me like that
I don't deserve it
How can I smooth out these edges
So I can just embrace you
Instead of waiting for you
to show me the real you
Don't love me like that
Is the real you what I've been seeing?
Just in case it isn't, though
Know I can't take another heartbreak
My heart won't last
So don't love me like that
I will just push you away
The more you come my way
because I don't deserve you
So don't love me like that
Save yourself

I Met a Man

I met a man
who never knew love
Love didn't grow where he grew
The love was never watered
so love died
long before it was supposed to
Due to no fault of his own
his version of love
turned into one-night stands
with countless women
organically or for a couple of dollars
It really didn't matter
because women weren't anything special
He just enjoyed the way they got him off
Offers of turning a casual relationship
into something serious were quite laughable
Comical, "you can't be serious" he would say
Expressing his disgust for how women were
and how he's better off alone than with anyone
But he ran into this woman from his past
That reconfigured his makeup
watered his garden
Love flourished where it hadn't before
I met a man, who now found
the thought of living without her comical
The thought of not making her his wife irresponsible

Rough Times

Rough times sometimes last
a long fucking time
Sometimes you want to give up
Sometimes you ask yourself, can it get any rougher?
And it sure fucking does
Sometimes you wish for that one break
to change your life
to change your luck
to turn your frown upside down
But most times you don't get that break
Most times you gotta hit rock bottom
be completely covered in dirt
buried alive
barely being able to breathe
But remember
seeds have to be buried completely in dirt
in order to grow
And before it sprouts
it's been growing in the dark
growing in the dirt
So whatever rough times you are going through right now
know it's part of your process of growth
You're gonna be just fine
You never ask a tree, "How did you get that big?"
Knowing it wasn't always as beautiful and majestic
It was once just a little seed in the dirt

The End

I have nothing left to say right now
Just know I left a piece of me
In the making of this book
In order to achieve peace
For all who read this
I'll bow now
and will forever be grateful
Thank you
Curtains close

ABOUT THE AUTHOR

A native New Yorker, MBA graduate, and former professional basketball player, Alejo A Rodriguez began his journey as an author by writing to express his innermost feelings and vulnerabilities which he felt he couldn't vocalize. Creating a collection of countless poems, Alejo struggled with the confidence to share them publicly and ultimately found himself destroying them.

Luckily, as time passed, his confidence grew stronger, and he allowed himself to be vulnerable, owning his form of expression and working to master his craft. His work became less about him and more about the ability to impact and empower others, helping them through the struggles of life. This collection is written from the heart with the hope that it touches the soul.

Enjoy!

CPSIA information can be obtained
at www.ICGtesting.com
Printed in the USA
BVHW030414150222
629060BV00002B/3